Making a New Nation

THE LOUISIANA PURCHASE
REVISED EDITION
From Independence to Lewis and Clark

Michael Burgan

capstone

Designed by Philippa Baile and Kim Miracle
Maps by Jeff Edwards

Library of Congress Cataloging-in-Publication Data is available on the Library of Congress website.
 ISBN 978-1-4846-3596-4 (paperback)

Acknowledgments
Alamy: ClassicStock, **19**, Interfoto, **35**; Art Resource, N.Y: Smithsonian American Art Museum, Washington, DC, **29**; Bridgeman Images/Peter Newark American Pictures: Paxson, Edgar Samuel, **26**, Russell, Charles Marion, **Cover**, Wyeth, Newell Convers, **5**; Getty Images: Bettmann, **33**, MPI, **15**; Granger, NYC: **38**; iStockphoto: Different_Brian, **41**, HultonArchive, **17**; Library of Congress: **7, 18**; National Archives and Records Administration: **24**; New York Public Library: Schomburg Center for Research in Black Culture, Jean Blackwell Hutson Research and Reference Division, **22**, The Miriam and Ira D. Wallach Division of Art, Prints and Photographs, **12, 42**; Newscom: BAO Image BROKER, **8**, Picture History, **25**; North Wind Picture Archives: **6, 10, 11, 27, 34**; Shutterstock: Everett Historical, **21**, J K Floyd, **31**, John R. McNair, **40**; SuperStock: Superstock, **43**; Thinkstock: GRAWLLF, **30**; Wikimedia: PD-USGOV-MILITARY-NAVY, **20**, The Indian Reporter, **9**, White House, **23**; Yale Collection of American Literature: Beinecke Rare Book and Manuscript Library, **28**

The publishers would like to thank David Davidson of Northwestern University for his help in the preparation of this book.

CONTENTS

Some words are shown in bold, **like this**. You can find out what they mean by looking in the glossary.

AN INDEPENDENT NATION

In 1775 Great Britain controlled much land in North America, including the thirteen **colonies** along the Atlantic Ocean. Some American **colonists** wanted more rights and did not like British taxes. American protests against British rule started the American Revolution. In 1776 colonial leaders declared **independence** from Great Britain and created the United States of America.

For six years, the Americans and British fought against each other. In 1781 the United States won a major victory in Yorktown, Virginia. British leaders then decided they should grant Americans their independence.

In 1787 Spanish land bordered the newly formed United States of America.

PEACE—AND NEW LANDS

After the war, the British and Americans discussed peace. Spain and France had been America's **allies** during the revolution, and they wanted to benefit from the peace **treaty**. Spain had its own colonies in other parts of North America, and it hoped to gain even more land. France was a close ally of Spain and an enemy of Great Britain. It wanted to help Spain become stronger in North America.

In 1783 the Americans and British signed the Treaty of Paris. In this peace treaty, Great Britain gave the United States all its land south of Canada as far west as the Mississippi River. The **borders** reached much farther west than the original thirteen colonies. Americans now had new lands they could freely settle and farm.

Battles in the Northwest

During the American Revolution, most of the battles were fought east of the Allegheny Mountains. These mountains stretch from Pennsylvania south to West Virginia. Some fighting, however, took place in land called the Old Northwest. This region was west of Pennsylvania and north of the Ohio River. In 1778 George Rogers Clark led troops in the Old Northwest against the British. In July 1778, the Americans took the town of Kaskaskia, in what is now Illinois. The next year, they captured Vincennes, in what is now Indiana.

The British surrendered to George Rogers Clark at Vincennes, in what is now Indiana, in 1779.

THE NORTHWEST TERRITORY

After the revolution, Americans had to decide how to govern their new western lands. Thomas Jefferson was a member of **Congress** from Virginia. He suggested dividing the Old Northwest into smaller **territories**. Each territory would be allowed to form its own government when its population reached 20,000. A territory could later become a state when its population matched that of the smallest of the original thirteen states.

Jefferson's proposal was called the Northwest Ordinance. However, it never went into effect. At the time, no U.S. **settlers** had lawfully moved into the Northwest Territory. The only people there were Native Americans, French-Canadian settlers, and **squatters**. Finally, in 1787 Congress approved a slightly different Northwest Ordinance. This gave the U.S. government control of the territories until their population reached 5,000 people. At that time, the people living in the territory were allowed to form a local government. When a territory had 60,000 people, it could become a state. The new Northwest Ordinance made owning **slaves** in the region against the law. It allowed settlers to worship as they chose.

Settlers cut down trees in the wilderness so they could farm and build homes.

In 1787 the United States was governed under the Articles of Confederation, which laid out the laws of the country. The Northwest Ordinance was possibly the most important law passed under the Articles. It created an orderly way to add new territories and states. This process was followed for more than a century. The ordinance also said that new states would have the same rights as the original thirteen states.

THOMAS JEFFERSON
President of the United States

As a scientist, Thomas Jefferson collected old animal bones from the mammoth, an ancestor of the elephant.

Jefferson and the West

Thomas Jefferson is best known today as the author of the Declaration of Independence and the third president. Jefferson was a scientist as well as a **political** leader. He was interested in the wildlife and geography of North America. He was curious about North America's western lands and was eager for explorations of the West to begin.

TRIBES OF THE NORTHWEST

In the late 1700s, the Northwest Territory was home to Native American **tribes** such as the Miami, Shawnee, Kickapoo, Lenni Lenape, and Chippewa. U.S. settlers had already forced some of these tribes from their lands in the East.

Under the Northwest Ordinance, Congress had promised that Native American lands and property would never be taken from them without their consent. In 1789 the new government formed under the U.S. Constitution said they would continue with this promise.

However, the policy had problems. It did not stop government officials and businesses from tricking Native Americans. Many Americans thought their freedom from the British also gave them the freedom to take whatever land they wanted. These people convinced the Native Americans to sign phony contracts that forced them to give up their lands.

Native American tribes built canoes out of birch and other types of wood.

THE BATTLE FOR LAND

Many tribes fought against the settlers in order to keep their lands. In 1790, in a series of attacks and battles, Native Americans killed as many as 1,500 people along the **frontier**. Finally, General Anthony Wayne led a 3,000-strong army large enough to crush the Native Americans. In 1795 the Native Americans chose to sign a peace treaty rather than continue the war. The tribes involved included the Shawnee, Delaware, Miami, Chippewa, and Kickapoo. The tribes gave up most of their lands in Ohio and part of their lands in Indiana. They stayed in the area, but could no longer hunt as before. This Treaty of Greenville made it easier for Americans to settle the Northwest Territory.

The Constitution

During the 1780s, leaders of the United States realized that the Articles of Confederation were not perfect. The Articles did not give Congress the power to collect taxes or end disputes between the states. The Constitution was created to give the country a stronger national government. The United States still uses the Constitution today.

Leaders of the United States met in Philadelphia in 1787 to create the Constitution.

TROUBLE WITH SPAIN

Now that the borders of the United States had increased, Americans began having more contact with the Spanish colonies. Spain controlled the mouth of the Mississippi River and the city of New Orleans. Under the Treaty of Paris, U.S. ships could sail freely to the mouth of the river and into the Gulf of Mexico. However, Spanish leaders did not want Americans settling near the river. To stop the **settlements**, they closed the **mouth** of the Mississippi to U.S. ships in 1784.

By this time, U.S. settlers had already begun to move to Kentucky and Tennessee. Farmers living there depended on the Mississippi to ship their goods to market. They were angry when Spain closed the river. Some even wanted to go to war.

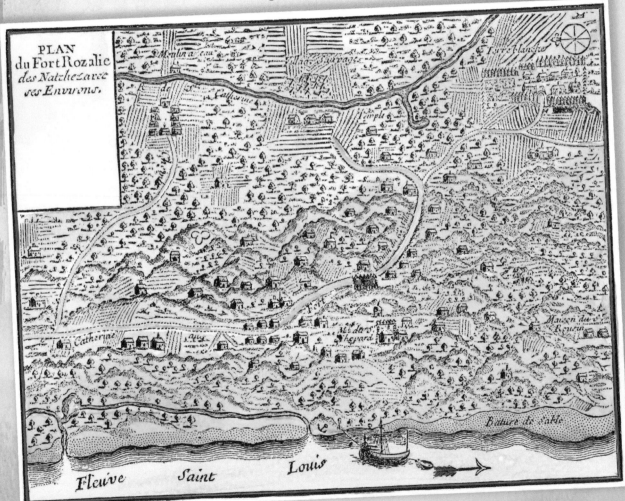

PLAN du Fort Rozalie des Natchez avec ses Environs.

This map from the 1700s shows Natchez, one of the major Spanish ports along the Mississippi River.

A PARTIAL VICTORY

U.S. and Spanish leaders hoped to avoid a war. In 1785 John Jay met with a Spanish **diplomat**. Jay was the U.S. **secretary** of foreign affairs. He suggested that Americans not use the Mississippi for 25 years. Spain said it would make up for the closing of the river by trading more with Americans. However, by 1787 the two sides had failed to solve the problem, and the talks ended. The next year, Spain let Americans use the river if they paid special taxes on the goods they shipped.

Spanish Louisiana

New Orleans and the mouth of the Mississippi River were located in what was called Spanish Louisiana. France had first settled the region in the early part of the 1700s. In 1763 French leaders gave the land to Spain. The land was a payment for Spanish help during the **French and Indian War**. For Spain, Louisiana was a **buffer** between the British colonists and rich lands in Mexico.

Settlers used large rowboats or barges to transport tobacco, grains, and other goods down the Mississippi River.

WAR PLANS

In 1793 the French decided they wanted more influence in Louisiana. A French diplomat gave money to George Rogers Clark, who had once been a U.S. general, to lead a private army and invade Louisiana. Clark believed that a victory in Louisiana would guarantee free access to the Mississippi River. Clark found about 2,000 soldiers, but France decided not to go ahead with the mission. The French did not want to anger the leaders of the United States. President George Washington had just declared that no Americans could fight against Spain. The threat of war in Louisiana, however, led to new talks between Spain and the United States.

Thomas Pinckney went to Spain in 1795 and helped to write Pinckney's Treaty, which gained use of the Mississippi for Americans.

Engᵈ by W. G. Armstrong from an original miniature in oil by J. Trumbull P.A.A.

MAJOR GENERAL THOMAS PINCKNEY.

Thomas Pinckney

TREATY WITH SPAIN

Since the American Revolution, relations between Great Britain and the United States had greatly improved. Furthermore, France and Spain were no longer allies, but were at war with each other in Europe. Spain did not want the Americans to be too friendly with the British or the French. Spain now wanted to improve its relations with the United States.

In 1795 Spain agreed to sign a treaty with the United States. The deal let the Americans freely use the Mississippi and bring their goods to New Orleans. The two countries also settled on the border between Spanish lands and the United States. Some Americans celebrated when they heard the news. They knew they could continue to expand westward and cheaply bring their goods to market.

Spy for Spain

Starting in 1787, Spain had an important U.S. spy helping its interests: James Wilkinson. He had served in the American Revolution and had hoped to make Kentucky an independent country. In attempting to do so, he sought Spanish help, and in return he gave them information about U.S. plans. While serving as a spy, Wilkinson commanded the U.S. Army in the western United States.

Territory lost by Spain at Pinckney's Treaty of 1795

Spanish territory after 1795

United States

British territory

This map shows the land Spain claimed in 1785 and the final border it accepted in 1795.

THE WESTERN FRONTIER

During the colonial era, most Americans lived close to the Atlantic Ocean. Even before the American Revolution, some headed west and south. Their numbers increased during the 1780s.

KENTUCKY AND TENNESSEE

In 1774 Daniel Boone began making a trail from Virginia to Kentucky. This route was later called the Wilderness Road. By 1800 it was used by more than 200,000 **pioneers** to settle lands south of the Northwest Territory. The first of these settlers lived in **forts**. Later, the settlers moved into their own homes. Some headed south, into Tennessee.

For the most part, settlers stayed close to rivers, such as the Ohio and Kentucky rivers. Rivers were important for transportation. Traveling through the woods by wagon was slow. It could also be dangerous because of Native American attacks. By the 1780s, small towns developed along these rivers, where merchants sold goods that farmers and hunters needed for their daily lives.

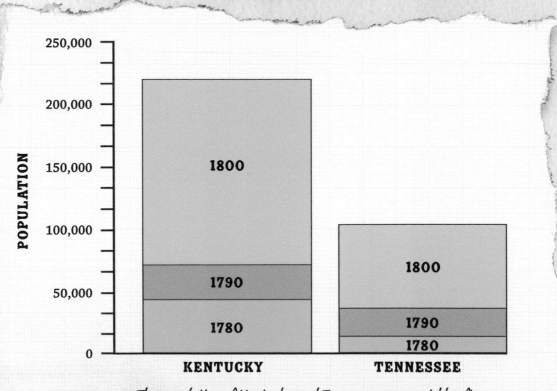

The population of Kentucky and Tennessee grew quickly after the arrival of the first U.S. settlers there in the 1770s.

Daniel Boone led settlers into Kentucky through the Cumberland Gap, a passage in the Appalachian Mountains.

Farms in this area were usually several miles apart. Even so, people worked together to build homes and clear fields for planting. Some people enjoyed the freedom of being on their own, away from the government and wealthy people who controlled life in the East. Farmers raised corn and vegetables to feed themselves and their families. For meat, many hunted turkey and deer.

A child's life

As a young boy during the 1780s and 1790s, Daniel Drake lived on the Kentucky frontier. As an adult, he described some of his daily chores:

"To chop, split, and bring in wood; keep up the fire ...were regular labors. To bring water from the spring, which was but a short distance from the house, was another. To slop [feed] the cows, and, when wild, drive them into a corner of the fence, and stand over them with a stick while mother milked them, was another."

THE NORTHWEST TERRITORY

To reward some soldiers for their service in the American Revolution, Congress gave them land in the Northwest Territory. The threat of Native American attacks had kept many people from moving there until after the Treaty of Greenville. Once the treaty was signed, settlers moved into the territory the tribes had agreed to give up. Even with the peace treaty, settlers and Native Americans sometimes fought each other.

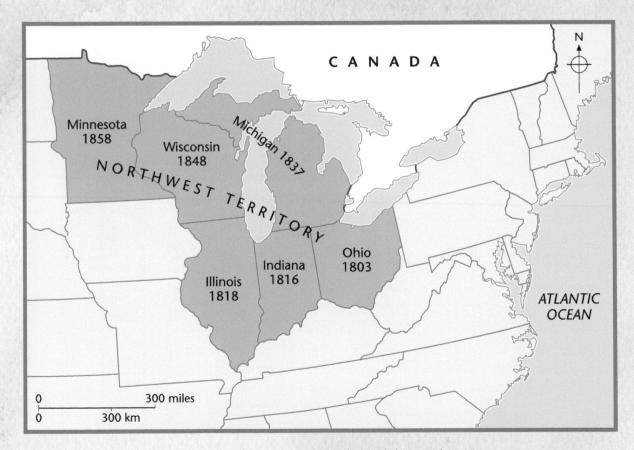

This map shows the states carved out of the Northwest Territory and the dates when they joined the Union.

MAKING A LIVING

Large groups of settlers went to Ohio. Some of the first major towns were Cleveland, Dayton, and Cincinnati. As in the southern frontier, settlers cleared land, built simple homes such as log cabins, and began to raise crops. Slavery was illegal in the Northwest, so the region attracted farmers and traders who did not own slaves. Slaveowners who had arrived in the Northwest Territory before the Northwest Ordinance of 1787 took effect were allowed to keep any slaves they had brought with them.

Farmers raised wheat and corn, among other crops. Some early settlers raised cattle. The setters also built mills to grind grain and turn trees into lumber. Farther west, in Michigan and Illinois, trappers looked for fur or traded for furs with Native Americans.

Runaway slaves

Slavery was illegal in the Northwest Territory. Settlers there were expected to return runaway slaves to their owners. Even so, some slaves from Kentucky and Tennessee crossed the Ohio River to the North and stayed there. During the early 1800s, Ohio and Indiana were the first important stops on the Underground Railroad. This "railroad" did not have tracks and trains. It was a system of people who helped runaway slaves.

MAJ. GEN. ARTHUR St CLAIR.

Arthur St. Clair was the first and only governor of the Northwest Territories, from 1787 to 1802.

LIFE IN LOUISIANA

When Spain acquired Louisiana in 1762, the region had few settlers. The capital and largest city was New Orleans. By 1788 it had about 5,000 people. That year, a huge fire swept through the city. The blaze destroyed most of the buildings there. Local officials quickly began rebuilding, so that trade and government could continue.

The white population of Louisiana was largely French. Living and working with the settlers were a large number of African-American slaves. They raised indigo, a plant used to make blue dye. Other crops grown in Louisiana included tobacco, cotton, and rice. Some of the citizens of New Orleans were called Creoles. This term referred to both blacks and whites born in Louisiana. *Creole* also refers to a language spoken in colonial Louisiana that combined French and West African words.

The Vieux Carré (French for "old quarter") was the first part of New Orleans settled by the French. The 1788 fire and another one six years later destroyed much of the Vieux Carré.

UPPER LOUISIANA

North of New Orleans was a region called Upper Louisiana. It included present-day Missouri. The first settlers in Upper Louisiana farmed and traded with the Native Americans for furs. In 1764 French settlers in the area crossed from the east bank of the Mississippi to the west bank and founded St. Louis. The fur trade was the main economic activity in St. Louis. The French settlers dealt with such Native American tribes as the Missouri and Osage.

Pierre Laclède, a French fur trader, and his stepson, Auguste Chouteau, founded St. Louis. They began by clearing land to build a trading post..

Cahokia

St. Louis was founded across the river from an old Native American settlement called Cahokia. Hundreds of years before Christopher Columbus sailed, Cahokia may have had about 10,000 residents. Both Cahokia and St. Louis sat at a spot where tribes from many regions came to trade furs and other goods.

BUYING LOUISIANA

Americans generally liked France and were thankful for France's aid during the American Revolution. Some Americans wanted to keep close ties with France when the war ended. Then, in 1789 France had its own revolution. France's new leaders governed harshly, killing many French people and France's former king. The bloodshed angered many Americans. France also started wars across Europe, and its warships sometimes seized U.S. merchant ships.

The U.S.S. Constellation *battles the* L'Insurgente *during the Quasi War.*

The Quasi War

French attacks on U.S. merchant ships led to the **Quasi** War between France and the United States. The two countries did not officially declare war. Still, between 1798 and 1800, French and U.S. warships battled each other in the Caribbean Sea. The treaty that ended the fighting was signed just one day before France made its secret deal to regain Louisiana from Spain.

FRANCE REGAINS LOUISIANA

In 1800 Napoleon Bonaparte was the ruler of France. He valued France's colonies in the **West Indies**. They produced sugar and coffee, two important crops sent to France. Napoleon saw that the old French territory of Louisiana could provide food for those colonies. Napoleon offered to trade Spain some land France had acquired in Italy for Louisiana. The Spanish agreed. They believed that France would do a better job of defending Louisiana from British or U.S. attack. The deal between France and Spain was secret, but U.S. diplomats in Europe learned about it in 1801.

Thomas Jefferson was now president of the United States. Jefferson knew how important the city of New Orleans was to shipping. He believed that U.S. settlers would someday live throughout Louisiana. The president also knew that France had a powerful army. Jefferson feared a war, but he had a plan for avoiding one. He hoped to buy New Orleans from France.

Napoleon Bonaparte was a brilliant general who helped France conquer much of Europe.

A CHANGING SITUATION

In the early 1800s, Great Britain was France's enemy. Jefferson hinted to the French that the United States would become friendlier with Great Britain if France took control of New Orleans. Napoleon did not want to see stronger ties between the British and Americans. By October 1802, Napoleon and his aides had decided to sell both New Orleans and Florida to the United States for $6 million, which would be worth about $102 million today.

France's situation in the West Indies then changed. Napoleon had sent a fleet of ships there to end a slave **rebellion**, but the rebels defeated the French. Napoleon changed his mind about the rest of Louisiana. France no longer needed it as a source of food for the West Indies. Selling all of Louisiana would keep the British from ever taking control of it. The sale would give even more money to use in fighting new wars.

Toussaint L'Ouverture led the slaves who rebelled in Santo Domingo against Napoleon's forces in the Caribbean. Today, Santo Domingo is called Haiti.

THE FINAL DEAL

James Monroe and Robert Livingston were the two U.S. diplomats who made the final deal with the French. They did not have orders to buy all of Louisiana. Still, they knew the deal was too good to pass up. On April 30, 1803, they bought Louisiana for $15 million. With the Louisiana Purchase, the United States doubled in size.

The question of Florida

The United States assumed that Spain's deal to give Louisiana back to France included Spanish Florida. The French themselves were not sure, and they could not tell the Americans if the Louisiana Purchase included Florida. In 1810 U.S. settlers seized a Spanish fort in West Florida (now part of the states of Louisiana and Mississippi). Two years later, the U.S. government officially made West Florida part of the United States. In 1819 the government bought the rest of Florida from Spain.

James Monroe served as a diplomat in Spain, Great Britain, and France before he was elected the fifth president of the United States in 1816.

FOES OF THE LOUISIANA PURCHASE

The details of the Louisiana Purchase reached the United States in the summer of 1803. Jefferson was thrilled, though he wondered if the deal was lawful. The Constitution did not specifically give a president the power to buy land from another nation. Some members of Congress were against the deal. Most of the critics belonged to the Federalist **Party**, which was centered in New England.

Many Federalists thought the government would not run well if the country was too big. Settlers in the West would lose contact with the business and political centers of the East. Other Federalists did not think the French and Spanish people of Louisiana would be able to govern themselves. They lacked experience with **democracy**, the form of government in the United States. Some people questioned the value of Louisiana. They said the country was paying too much for it. One newspaper in Boston called the land a great waste. But most Americans were pleased with the new land.

The treaty for the Louisiana Purchase and other documents related to it are kept in the Library of Congress in Washington, D.C.

THE AMERICANS TAKE CONTROL

Despite these concerns, Congress approved the Louisiana Purchase. On December 20, 1803, General James Wilkinson led U.S. troops into New Orleans, and France formally gave Louisiana to the United States. A similar ceremony was later held in St. Louis and two other towns. Some French citizens cried as the Americans took over, but the exchange was peaceful. The expansion of the United States westward would continue.

Louisiana Territory facts

Size: 529,911,680 acres (214,447,649 hectares)
Cost per acre: Less than 5 cents
Population: 50,000 settlers (mostly French) and 150,000 Native Americans
Major cities and forts in 1803: New Orleans, St. Louis, Natchitoches, New Madrid

In 1803 the population of New Orleans (shown here) was about 8,500. This included about 2,800 slaves and 1,300 free African Americans.

UNDER MY WINGS EVERY THING PROSPERS

CAPTAINS OF DISCOVERY

Americans had started to explore Louisiana in the 1780s and 1790s. Thomas Jefferson wanted the government to send its own **expedition** to explore the area of the Louisiana Purchase. He wanted to trade with Native Americans west of the Mississippi River. Early in 1803, Congress approved the request, and Jefferson chose Captain Meriwether Lewis to lead the western expedition.

In June, Jefferson gave Lewis specific instructions. He and a small group of men were to explore the Missouri River, which ran into the Mississippi. Their goal was to find the best water route to the Pacific Ocean. Along the way, the men would meet with Native American tribes. Lewis should learn about how they lived and what the Americans could trade with them. Jefferson also had other tasks for Lewis. He was to look for **minerals** and write about unusual plants and animals he saw. Jefferson also wanted him to keep track of the weather. Jefferson told Lewis to keep careful notes.

Lewis (center) was 28 years old and Clark was 32 when they took command of the Corps of Discovery.

FIRST PLANS

Lewis asked William Clark to share the duties of leading the expedition. Clark accepted. The two men then began building their team, called the **Corps** of Discovery. Lewis bought supplies in Philadelphia. He also bought presents to give to the tribes the Corps would meet. These included metal pots and knives. Both men recruited others to join their bold expedition.

Meriwether Lewis and William Clark

During the 1790s, Meriwether Lewis served in the U.S. Army in the Northwest Territory. In 1801 Thomas Jefferson hired him as his private secretary. Jefferson chose Lewis for the western expedition because of his knowledge of the frontier and his military skills. William Clark had met Meriwether Lewis while serving in the army. Clark was an experienced officer who could act coolly during a crisis.

Clark wrote three different letters to Lewis agreeing to go on the mission. He wanted to make sure at least one reached Lewis.

MEETING IN ST. LOUIS

In December 1803, Lewis and Clark arrived in St. Louis, before spending the winter on the other side of the Mississippi River, in Illinois. In May 1804, the Corps of Discovery began its journey by crossing the Mississippi and entering the Missouri River.

The expedition was made up of about 48 men. They sailed in one **keelboat** and two canoes. While sailing along the Missouri River, the Corps passed Native Americans sailing downriver with boatloads of furs to trade. The men also saw a few scattered buildings on shore. These were the homes of French and U.S. pioneers. One of the homes belonged to Daniel Boone.

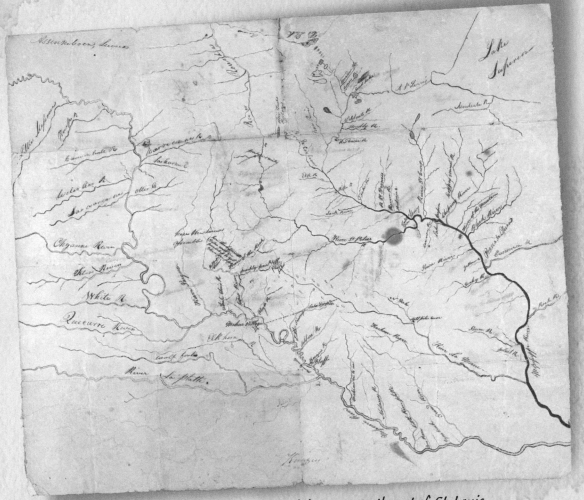

William Clark drew this map of the area Northwest of St. Louis in 1803. He made more than 100 maps during the expedition.

LIFE ON THE RIVER

At first the men sailed west. Then, the Missouri River turned north, toward the Dakotas. Their trip now took them into the Great Plains. This region is a mostly flat, treeless stretch between the Missouri River and the Rocky Mountains. Some days, the Corps came ashore and explored the land. At night, the men camped in tents along the riverbank. They hunted deer, buffalo, and fished in the river. The Corps also had a kind of paste called portable soup. This mixture of beef and vegetables was not very tasty. Lewis kept it only for emergencies.

On their journey, the men saw animals they had never seen before. These included pronghorn antelope and prairie dogs, which Clark called ground rats.

The Corps of Discovery

The men who sailed with Lewis and Clark included soldiers and French **civilians**. One member of the Corps was George Drouillard, a half-French, half-Native American guide. He helped the Americans speak with Native Americans they met along the way. Clark's African-American slave, York, helped the men hunt and served as a scout. Clark also brought his dog, Seaman.

This painting, by expedition artist George Catlin, shows where Sergeant Charles Floyd was buried. He was the only member of Corps to die during the expedition.

From Clark's journal

August 24 "[Found] great quantities of a kind of berry resembling a currant except double the size. It grows on a bush.... Killed two buck elks and a fawn and...had all the meat butchered and in by sunset, at which time it began to rain."

WINTER REST

By October 1804, the Corps of Discovery reached present-day North Dakota. The men then built Fort Mandan. They named it for a Native American tribe that lived in the region. The Corps lived at the fort during the winter. At times, the temperatures plunged as low as −45° F (−43° C). Clark was amazed at how well the Mandan coped with the bitter cold. In April 1805, the Corps began chopping at the ice that still surrounded their boats. The keelboat returned to St. Louis with some of the men. They took with them the animal **specimens** the Corps had found so far. The rest of the Corps continued to head west.

The Corps ran into a series of waterfalls called the Great Falls. The men carried boats and supplies more than 18 miles (29 km) to get around them.

ACROSS THE MOUNTAINS

The Corps faced some difficulties along this stretch of the Missouri River. One boat tipped on its side and almost sank. Luckily, only a few items were lost in the river. One night, a buffalo stomped through the camp and almost killed several men. Food was running low, and strong winds in their faces made it hard for the men to paddle upstream.

By June, Lewis and Clark reached the Rocky Mountains. They were the first U.S. citizens to see these peaks. They had to **navigate** a series of waterfalls. After trekking through more mountains, they reached the Snake River. From there, they sailed along the Columbia River.

In the Rocky Mountains, Lewis and Clark crossed the Continental Divide. West of the divide, rivers flow westward. East of it, rivers flow eastward.

The Corps at play

During their trip, the Corps of Discovery took time to rest and enjoy themselves. At Fort Mandan, the men danced and sang. They had brought a fiddle and tambourine with them. At times they entertained the Native Americans they met with their music. The explorers also played a game called base, which was loosely related to baseball.

HELP ALONG THE WAY

A new guide helped lead the Corps as it traveled west from the Great Falls. Sacagawea was a Shoshone. She and her French-Canadian husband, Toussaint Charbonneau, had joined the expedition at Fort Mandan. Sacagawea was one of many Native Americans who helped Lewis and Clark survive as they traveled west.

At Fort Mandan, the Americans had traded with the Mandan tribe for corn. The Mandan also showed them their methods for hunting buffalo. Members of other tribes gave the explorers maps. They also told them about landmarks they would see on their journey. Before 1804, no white Americans had crossed the Great Plains into the Rockies. Yet many Native Americans had. They knew all about the region and its geography.

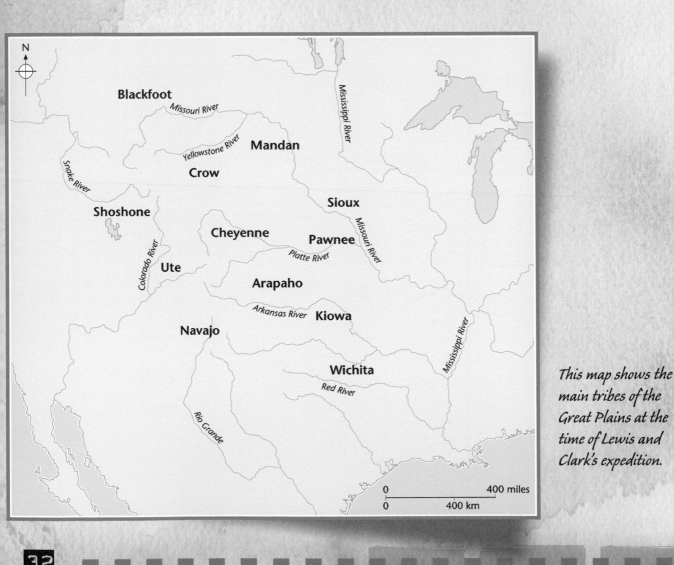

This map shows the main tribes of the Great Plains at the time of Lewis and Clark's expedition.

DIPLOMACY

Close to St. Louis, the Native American tribes were familiar with white men. French and Spanish traders had been in that region for many years. Farther west, however, the tribes had never seen Europeans or African Americans. For the most part, the tribes were friendly, but not everything went smoothly. Lewis and Clark had some trouble with the Teton Sioux of South Dakota. The Americans spent four days with the Sioux, trying to build good relations. They gave the tribe's leaders medals and clothing as gifts. The Sioux demanded more, and Clark drew his sword. He feared that the arguing over gifts might lead to violence. The Corps left without a peace treaty with the Sioux.

Sacagawea's son Jean-Baptiste was born in Fort Mandan and he, too, came along on the expedition. During the trip, Sacagawea helped look for food and also served as a guide.

Deadly disease

During the 1770s, a smallpox **epidemic** struck the Native American tribes of the West. The first Europeans had brought this deadly disease to North America. Some of the tribes Lewis and Clark met said whole villages were wiped out by smallpox.

TO THE PACIFIC AND BACK

As Lewis and Clark traveled the Snake and Columbia rivers, they met more Native American tribes. These included the Yakama, Palouse, and Flathead. In November, the Corps of Discovery finally reached its final goal, the Pacific Ocean. The men explored the coast for several weeks. They then moved south of the Columbia River.

Winter was approaching, so once again the men built a fort. They named it after the Clatsop, a tribe that lived nearby. Rain fell throughout the winter. The men passed their time hunting and preparing for the trip home. The clothes and shoes they had brought had worn out, so they made new ones out of elk skin.

Clark drew this salmon. He copied it from a real one that was almost 3 feet (1 meter) long.

HEADING HOME

In March the Corps left Fort Clatsop. They started back the way they had come. Along the way, the Americans lost several canoes, and they did not have horses. They had left theirs with the Nez Perce tribe months before, because the land was too rough for the animals to cross. Now, the Americans bought new horses from tribes they met along the Columbia River.

In May, the men returned to the Nez Perce village they had visited on their way out. They stayed there several weeks. They waited for the snow to melt so they could safely pass through the mountains. They crossed the Bitterroot Range, which is part of the Rockies. Lewis and Clark then decided to explore separate routes.

Lewis bought a medicine chest similar to this one for the expedition.

Medical help

Throughout the expedition, the Americans and Native Americans shared their medical knowledge. Lewis had brought several drugs with him that the Native Americans had never seen. One of them was opium, which kills pain. The tribes often used steam baths to heal illness and pain. A Native American steam bath cured Corps member William Bratton's severe back pain.

TROUBLE ON THE RIVER

With Sacagawea's help, Clark led some of the men down the Yellowstone River. Meanwhile, Lewis and his group took a shortcut to the Great Falls and the Missouri River. They then headed north, traveling near the present-day border with Canada. In late July, Lewis met members of the Blackfeet tribe. They tried to rob the Americans. The two sides fired at each other, and two Blackfeet were killed. They were the only Native American **casualties** during the expedition. A few weeks later, the Americans had their own casualty, when Lewis was accidentally shot by one of his own men. Luckily, the wound was not serious.

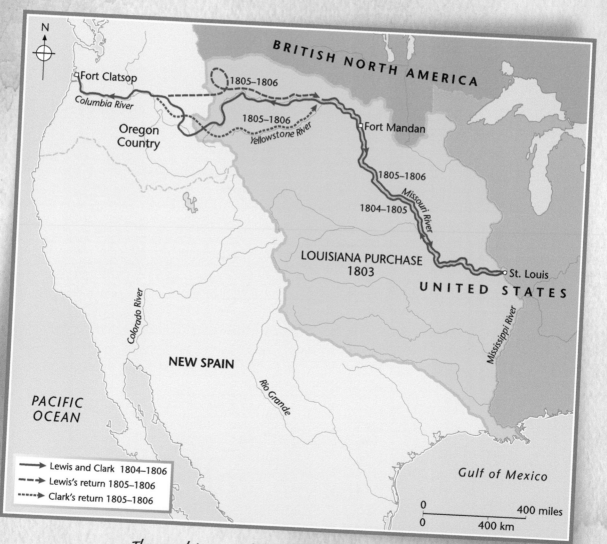

The complete route of the Lewis and Clark expedition went to the Pacific Ocean and back to St. Louis.

THE LAST LEG

Lewis and Clark soon reunited west of Fort Mandan. The Corps had faced two years of harsh weather and rough terrain. All the men were now eager to return to St. Louis. The Corps was now traveling with the current of the Missouri River. This made sailing easy, and at times they covered 70 miles (113 kilometers) a day. Nearing St. Louis, they saw boats carrying traders up the river. One captain told the men that most Americans assumed the Corps had been lost and would never return. When the men reached St. Louis, the citizens cheered.

President Jefferson said he felt "unspeakable joy" after learning Lewis and Clark had returned. Newspapers praised the men and their mission. Soon, many of the items Lewis and Clark gathered went on display at a Philadelphia museum. In 1807 Corps member Patrick Gass published his journal from the trip. It was popular all over the world.

Discoveries of the expedition

Here are some of the animals Lewis and Clark brought home with them or shipped home during the expedition:

- Magpie (live)
- Prairie dog (live)
- Sea otter (skin)
- Bighorn sheep (skin)
- Horned toad (live, but soon died)
- Bear (skin)
- Lewis's woodpecker (dead)

1803

Thomas Jefferson chooses Meriwether Lewis to lead an expedition west.

1804

March
St. Louis and the rest of Upper Louisiana become U.S. territory.

May
The Corps of Discovery leaves St. Louis.

October
The men begin building their winter quarters, Fort Mandan.

November
Sacagawea and her husband join the expedition.

1805

April
The trip resumes up the Missouri River.

June
The Corps reaches the Great Falls.

August
The expedition crosses the Continental Divide.

November
The Corps reaches the Pacific Ocean.

1806

March
The return trip home begins.

July
The Corps splits into two groups. Lewis and his men kill two Blackfeet.

August
The two groups reunite.

September
The Corps returns to St. Louis.

Major events of the Lewis and Clark expedition included Sacagawea joining the expedition and the Corps reaching the Pacific Ocean.

OTHER EXPLORATIONS

In 1804 President Jefferson sent other explorers into the southern part of the Louisiana Territory. Scientists William Dunbar and George Hunter led an expedition down the Mississippi River. They then sailed up the Ouachita River into what is now Arkansas. They met French and American hunters and traders as well as Native Americans. Like Lewis and Clark, Hunter and Dunbar noted the plants, animals, and minerals they saw. They finished their expedition in early 1805.

This painting, by expedition artist George Catlin, shows the Osage hunting buffalo for their meat and skin. They used buffalo bones for tools.

THE GRAND EXPEDITION

Jefferson planned another mission that he called the Grand Expedition or the Grand Excursion. The border between the Louisiana Territory and Spanish lands of New Mexico was unclear. The United States and Spain disagreed about the border. Before settling the border issues with the Spanish, Jefferson wanted to know as much as possible about the lands in the area.

Jefferson chose Thomas Freeman, Peter Custis, and Captain Richard Sparks to lead the expedition. They left in early 1806 with about twenty men. Once again, Jefferson wanted the explorers to learn about the geography and the Native Americans of the region. He hoped that one day Americans would settle in those lands.

This map shows the major rivers and towns of the southwestern corner of the Louisiana Territory and the nearby Spanish lands.

The Osage

On their southwestern expeditions, the Americans entered the land of the Osage. This tribe controlled land south of the Missouri River. It gradually spread its influence into Arkansas. The Osage hunted buffalo, just as the Great Plains tribes did. The Osage sought more land and wanted to control trade. These desires led to clashes with the Spanish and other Native Americans in the region. The Osage's fierce warriors slowed U.S. settlement in Arkansas.

MORE SPANISH TROUBLE

Spain knew about the Grand Expedition. It did not want Americans exploring what it considered Spanish lands. Spain sent troops to prevent Freeman and the others from advancing. In July 1806, these forces waited for the Americans at a spot called Spanish Bluff. Outnumbered, the Americans chose to turn back.

Pike called this peak in the Colorado Rockies "Blue Mountain," but it was later named "Pike's Peak."

PIKE'S MISSION

While the Grand Expedition was coming to an end, another southwestern expedition was already underway. In 1805 General James Wilkinson was named governor of the Louisiana Territory. The next year, he picked Zebulon Pike to explore the Red River.

Pike and his team first traveled up the Arkansas River before crossing the Rocky Mountains. In northern New Mexico, Pike built a fort at what he thought was the head of the Red River. Instead, he had ended up along the **Rio** Grande. He was in the heart of Spanish lands. Spanish troops soon arrested Pike and his men and took them to Mexico. Spanish officials took Pike's papers. They then sent him and the other Americans back to Louisiana.

None of the three southwestern expeditions were as successful as Lewis and Clark's. But they showed the Americans' great interest in continuing to expand their country's borders.

The Red River starts in eastern New Mexico and flows into the Mississippi. It covers a distance of just over 1,000 miles (1,609 kilometers).

41

LOOKING AHEAD

After the Louisiana Purchase, Thomas Jefferson focused on settling the lands east of the Mississippi River. The president wanted to buy land from the Native Americans there and send the tribes to the new lands of Louisiana. The government would then sell the Native Americans' old lands to settlers. But Jefferson knew the lands east of the Mississippi would quickly fill with Americans. Jefferson said the United States would then create "a range of States on the Western bank from the head to the mouth." The tribes would once again be forced from their lands.

In 1811 John Jacob Astor built Fort Astoria. It was the first U.S. trading post near the Pacific Ocean, in Oregon.

TRADING IN THE WEST

U.S. traders did not wait for settlers to arrive before starting to trade in the West. They knew the West was rich with furs. William Clark was a partner in a company that launched a fur-trading expedition in 1809. Jefferson also supported efforts to build trading forts between St. Louis and the Pacific coast. The War of 1812 between the United States and Great Britain slowed these plans. But when the war ended in 1815, the United States would once again prepare to explore and settle the West.

The Trail of Tears

Some Cherokee of Georgia were among the first Native Americans to sell their lands and move west. They settled in Arkansas. By 1810 about 1,000 Cherokee had moved. A treaty signed in 1817 gave the Cherokee even more land in Arkansas, and several thousand more arrived. By the 1830s, all the Cherokee who wanted to leave Georgia had done so. President Andrew Jackson, however, wanted more land for settlers in Georgia. He forced the Cherokee and other tribes to move to Oklahoma. Many Cherokee died during this forced move. The survivors called the experience the Trail of Tears.

On the Trail of Tears, many Cherokee traveled 1,000 miles (1,609 km) by land to Oklahoma. Others took boats for part of their journey.

CHART OF NEW STATES

Between 1803 and 1912, a total of twenty new states were carved out of the Northwest Territory and the Louisiana Purchase. This chart shows those states and their capitals.

STATE	YEAR ENTERED UNION	CAPITAL	PART OF
Arkansas	1836	Little Rock	LA Purchase
Colorado	1876	Denver	LA Purchase
Illinois	1818	Springfield	NW Territory
Indiana	1816	Indianapolis	NW Territory
Iowa	1846	Des Moines	LA Purchase
Kansas	1861	Topeka	LA Purchase
Louisiana	1812	Baton Rouge	LA Purchase
Michigan	1837	Lansing	NW Territory
Minnesota	1858	St. Paul	both
Missouri	1821	Jefferson City	LA Purchase
Montana	1889	Helena	LA Purchase
Nebraska	1867	Lincoln	LA Purchase
New Mexico	1912	Santa Fe	LA Purchase
North Dakota	1889	Bismarck	LA Purchase
Ohio	1803	Columbus	NW Territory
Oklahoma	1907	Ok. City	LA Purchase
South Dakota	1889	Pierre	LA Purchase
Texas	1845	Austin	LA Purchase
Wisconsin	1848	Madison	NW Territory
Wyoming	1890	Cheyenne	LA Purchase

TIMELINE

1783 Great Britain grants the United States its independence. The Americans receive British land north of the Ohio River and east of the Mississippi and call it the Northwest Territory.

1784 Spain closes the mouth of the Mississippi River to U.S. ships.

1787 Congress passes the Northwest Ordinance. This law spells out how new states will be formed in the Northwest Territory.

1788 U.S. ships can once again sail to the mouth of the Mississippi and unload cargo in New Orleans.

1789 The U.S. Constitution takes effect.

1790 War breaks out between the United States and Native Americans of the Northwest Territory.

1795 The Treaty of Greenville ends the war with Native Americans in the Northwest Territory. The peace leads to the opening up large parts of land to settlers. Pinckney's Treaty ends border and trade disputes between Spain and the United States.

1798–1800 "Quasi War" between France and the United States is fought at sea.

1800 Spain secretly agrees to trade Louisiana to France for French lands in Italy.

1801 President Thomas Jefferson learns about the Spanish trading Louisiana with the French and hopes to buy Louisiana from France.

1802 France loses a slave rebellion in Santo Domingo, a colony in the West Indies, and no longer needs Louisiana.

1803 France agrees to sell all of Louisiana to the United States for $15 million.
Meriwether Lewis and William Clark prepare for their expedition along the Missouri River to the Pacific Ocean.

1804 Lewis and Clark leave St. Louis and spend the winter at Fort Mandan, North Dakota. Jefferson sends another expedition to explore the Ouachita River, in the southwest corner of the Louisiana Territory.

1805 Lewis and Clark reach the Pacific Ocean.

1806 The Lewis and Clark expedition returns to St. Louis. Two expeditions attempt to explore the Red River. One is turned back by Spanish forces. On the other, Zebulon Pike crosses the Rocky Mountains and reaches the Rio Grande before the Spanish also force him back.

1811 John Jacob Astor opens a trading post in Oregon.

1812 The United States and Great Britain begin the War of 1812.

1815 The War of 1812 ends.

GLOSSARY

ally person or country working with another for a common goal, such as defeating an enemy

border dividing line between one country or region and another

buffer land that serves to prevent enemies from reaching more important territory

casualty person killed or wounded in battle

cede to give up power or land

civilian person who is not in the military

colonist someone who lives in a newly settled area

colony land not connected to a nation yet owned and controlled by it

Congress part of the U.S. government that makes the country's laws

corps group of people assembled for a task

democracy form of government in which citizens make political decisions as a group, or elect others to make those decisions

diplomat person who represents his or her country in a foreign nation

epidemic when a disease affects many people in one particular area for a short time

expedition trip taken for a specific reason, such as to explore unknown lands; also, the people who take such a trip

fort building that is strongly built to withstand or survive attacks

French and Indian War war fought in North America from 1754 to 1763 between Great Britain and France. Key Native Americans tribes fought on the same side as the French.

frontier largely unsettled border areas of a region or colony

independence freedom from another person's or country's control

keelboat covered boat that can travel through shallow water

mineral substance found in the ground that can be made into products

mouth part of a river where it enters the ocean

navigate to guide a ship in a certan direction using maps and instruments

party group of people who share the same political views and goals

pioneer first person to do something, especially settle in a particular region

political relating to the government and how it runs

quasi similar but not exactly like something else

rebellion effort to change a government using violence

rio Spanish word for *river*

secretary person who leads a government department

settlement colony or group of people who have left one place to make a home in another

settler person who moves from one place into a new region

slave person forced to work for others and do whatever they demand

specimen sample of a plant, animal, or substance

squatter person who lives on land he or she does not own

territory area of land

treaty written agreement between two countries or groups

tribe group of people who share the same ancestors, customs, and laws

West Indies group of islands in the Caribbean Sea, located south of Florida and north of South America

FURTHER READING

BOOKS

Behrman, Carol H. *The Indian Wars*. Minneapolis: Lerner, 2005.

Blumberg, Rhoda. *York's Adventures with Lewis and Clark*. New York: HarperCollins Children's Books, 2004.

Cook, Diane. *Pathfinders of the American Frontier*. Philadelphia: Mason Crest, 2003.

Isserman, Maurice. *Across America: The Lewis and Clark Expedition*. New York: Facts on File, 2005.

Koestler-Grack, Rachel A. *Sacagawea*. Chicago: Heinemann Library, 2004.

Kukla, Amy and John. *Thomas Jefferson: Life, Liberty, and the Pursuit of Happiness*. New York: PowerPlus, 2005.

Ray, Kurt. *Native Americans and the New American Government: Treaties and Promises*. New York: Rosen, 2004.

Smithyman, Kathryn, and Bobbie Kalman. *Nations of the Northwest Coast*. New York: Crabtree, 2004.

Stout, Mary. *Nez Perce*. Milwaukee: Gareth Stevens/World Almanac, 2003.

Teitelbaum, Michael. *The U.S. Constitution*. Chanhassen, Minn.: Child's World, 2005.

INTERNET

Kentucky Migration and Settlement
http://www.wku.edu/Library/museum/education/frontieronline/frontiermigration.htm

Jefferson's West
http://www.monticello.org/jefferson/lewisandclark

Lewis and Clark—The Journey of the Corps of Discovery
http://www.pbs.org/lewisandclark/

National Lewis and Clark Bicentennial Commemoration
http://www.lewisandclark200.org

The Northwest Ordinance
http://usinfo.state.gov/usa/infousa/facts/democrac/5.htm

Thomas Jefferson—The West
http://www.loc.gov/exhibits/jefferson/jeffwest.html

INDEX